# THE OFFICIAL

# RANGERS
## FOOTBALL CLUB

# ANNUAL 2018

### Written by Paul Kiddie
### Designed by Jon Dalrymple

A Grange Publication

© 2017. Published by Grange Communications Ltd., Edinburgh, under licence from Rangers Football Club. Printed in the EU.

Photographs © PA Images

ISBN 978-1-911287-79-7

# Contents

# Roll of Honour

## European Cup Winners' Cup

Winners 1972;
Runners-up 1961, 1967

## UEFA Cup

Runners-up 2008

## Scottish League Champions (54)

*1891, 1899, 1900, 1901, 1902, 1911, 1912, 1913, 1918, 1920, 1921, 1923, 1924, 1925, 1927, 1928, 1929, 1930, 1931, 1933, 1934, 1935, 1937, 1939, 1947, 1949, 1950, 1953, 1956, 1957, 1959, 1961, 1963, 1964, 1975, 1976, 1978, 1987, 1989, 1990, 1991, 1992, 1993, 1994, 1995, 1996, 1997, 1999, 2000, 2003, 2005, 2009, 2010, 2011

*In 1891 the championship was shared with Dumbarton

## Scottish Cup Winners (33)

1894, 1897, 1898, 1903, 1928, 1930, 1932, 1934, 1935, 1936, 1948, 1949, 1950, 1953, 1960, 1962, 1963, 1964, 1966, 1973, 1976, 1978, 1979, 1981, 1992, 1993, 1996, 1999, 2000, 2002, 2003, 2008, 2009

## Scottish League Cup Winners (27)

Season Starting: 1946, 1948, 1960, 1961, 1963, 1964, 1970, 1975, 1977, 1978, 1981, 1983, 1984, 1986, 1987, 1988, 1990, 1992, 1993, 1996, 1998, 2001, 2002, 2004, 2007, 2009, 2010

## SPFL Championship Winners (1)

2016

## SPFL League One Winners (1)

2014

## Scottish League Three Winners (1)

2013

## Record Ibrox Attendance

118,730 v Celtic, Division One, January 2, 1939

## Record Victory

13-0 v Possilpark, Scottish Cup, October 6, 1877;
v Uddingston, Scottish Cup,
November 10, 1877 and v Kelvinside,
Scottish Cup, September 28, 1889

## Most Goals in a Game

14-2 Blairgowrie, Scottish Cup, 1934

## Record League Defeat

1-7 v Celtic, League Cup Final,
October 19, 1957

## Record League Victory

10-0 v Hibs, December 24, 1898

## Record League Defeat

0-6 v Dumbarton, May 4, 1892

## Record Appearances

Dougie Gray, 948, 1925-47

## Record League Appearances

Sandy Archibald, 513, 1917-34

## Record Scottish Cup Appearances

Alec Smith, 74

## Record League Cup Appearances

John Greig, 121

## Record European Appearances

Barry Ferguson 82

## Record Scorer

Ally McCoist 355 goals, 1983-98

## Highest Number of Goals in a Season

Jim Forrest, 57 goals in 1964-65

## Highest Number of League Goals in a Season

Sam English, 44 goals in 1931-32

## Most League Goals

Ally McCoist, 251

## Most Scottish Cup Goals

Jimmy Fleming, 44

## Most League Cup Goals

Ally McCoist, 55

## Most European Goals

Ally McCoist, 21

## Most Capped Player While At Rangers

Ally McCoist (61 caps for Scotland)

## Record Transfer Fee Received

£9million received for Alan Hutton

## Record Transfer Fee Paid

£12million paid for Tore Andre Flo

# Player Profiles

## WES FODERINGHAM

Rangers secured the signing of goalkeeper Wes Foderingham on a three year deal, with an option for a fourth year, in July 2015, the keeper being ever-present in his first year at the club as Rangers secured the Championship in style. The 6ft 1in shot-stopper left Swindon Town after his contract expired and Gers batted away interest from a number of English clubs to seal the 24 year old's signature. Wes spent four years at the County Ground, making over 150 appearances for The Robins and impressed as the team were promoted by winning League Two in his first season. He started his career at Fulham before signing his first professional contract with Crystal Palace in August 2010. He was loaned out to a number of lower league clubs to gain experience before moving to Swindon and never returning to Palace, such was his impact with Town.

## JAK ALNWICK

The former England Under-18 international penned a three and a half year contract January 2017 after arriving from Port Vale. Alnwick made 67 appearances for the Valiants where he moved in August 2015. The 6ft 2in stopper started his career at Sunderland before moving to local rivals Newcastle United to continue his development. It was under Alan Pardew that Alnwick made his first-team debut for the Magpies as a substitute for the injured Rob Elliot in a 2-1 win over Chelsea at St James' Park. He impressed and was handed his full debut a week later against Arsenal. With both of Newcastle's first-team keepers fit again, Alnwick was loaned out to Bradford City but made just one appearance for the Yorkshire club before making a permanent move to Port Vale. Alnwick was capped by England at Under-17 and Under-18 levels and was named in the squad for the 2011 FIFA Under-20 World Cup in Colombia as back-up to Jack Butland and Lee Nicholls.

## LIAM KELLY

Goalkeeper Liam Kelly penned a new two year contract at Ibrox in June 2017. The young shot-stopper, who came through the youth ranks at Auchenhowie, spent the last season and a half on loan at East Fife and Livingston respectively, and has impressed boss Pedro Caixinha sufficiently to be rewarded with his new deal. Indeed, having won League Two with the Fifers, he was a near ever-present for Livi last season as they claimed the League One title in some style, while previously he played key roles in penalty shootout wins for Gers' youth sides in the 2012 Glasgow Cup and 2014 Youth Cup. Kelly has also represented Scotland at a variety of age groups, most recently the Under-21 side. He is a well-known face to supporters having been back-up to Wes Foderingham for the first half of the 2015/16 season and will be looking to make an impression over the next 18 months or so.

## LEE WALLACE

Lee Wallace has proved himself as Mr Dependable since joining from Hearts in July 2011 for a fee of £1.5 million. He managed his first Old Firm goal with a fabulous finish in Rangers' sensational 3-2 victory over Celtic in March 2012. He was then the first high profile star to commit his future to the Light Blues following the administration episode. He was promoted to Vice Captain as Rangers began life in the Third Division, and showed his true quality by creating a trademark of charging runs from left back. Now Captain, he leads by example every week. Consistent and strong, Lee made his first full international appearance against Japan in October 2009, having previously represented Scotland at Under-19, Under-20 and Under-21 levels.

## MYLES BEERMAN

The teenager arrived at Ibrox in August 2016 after leaving Manchester City in search of first-team football. His decision soon proved to be the correct one with the defender making his debut against Kilmarnock some eight months later. He went on to earn a run of games towards the end of last season as a replacement for the injured Lee Wallace and will be hoping for more opportunities as a member of the Ibrox first-team set-up. A Maltese international, he made his debut for his country as a substitute in a surprise 1-0 victory over Ukraine in a friendly in June.

## BRUNO ALVES

The experienced defender became Pedro Caixinha's first signing in the summer, penning a two year deal. The Portuguese centre half has enjoyed a glittering career at club level and with his national team. A player with a strong character and winning mentality, Alves started his career at Porto and had loan spells with Farense, Vitória de Guimarães and AEK Athens before returning to the Dragons and cementing his place in their first-team. From there he bagged nine major honours, including four league titles, before he joined Zenit Saint Petersburg in August 2010 for £22 million. In Russia he won two Premier League titles and the country's Super Cup before agreeing to move to Turkish side Fenerbahçe in June 2013 for a reported fee of £5.5 million. In his first season in Istanbul he helped the club win the Süper Lig and the Turkish Super Cup before signing for Serie A side Cagliari. He was in the winning Portugal squad during the European Championships in France, his country's first ever major trophy, playing in the 2-0 semi-final victory over Wales.

## FÁBIO CARDOSO

The Portuguese centre half joined the Light Blues from Vitória Setubal in his homeland. A former youth and Under-20 star with Portugal, Cardoso started his career with Benfica and played for their 'B' team before going on loan to another Primeira Liga side, Paços de Ferreira, in January 2015. He then moved to Setúbal in July 2016, having agreed a four year contract, and in 2016/17 made 23 appearances for the club. Another highly-rated defender from Portugal, Cardoso is a commanding and powerful figure who is comfortable on the ball.

## DANNY WILSON

He rejoined Rangers in the summer of 2015 on a three year deal, five years after departing Ibrox for Liverpool. The defender returned to the Light Blues after two and a half seasons with Hearts. He captained the Edinburgh club to the Championship title in 2014/15. In his first spell with Rangers, Wilson made his debut as a 17 year old. He left Ibrox having played his part in securing both the league title and the League Cup. Wilson also collected a Scottish Cup medal the previous season after spending the 1-0 win over Falkirk among the unused subs. Injury ruled him out of the run-in to last season. His international career involves caps for Scotland from Under-17 level right through to the full national side.

# Player Profiles

## DAVID BATES

The boyhood Rangers fan signed in January 2017 having originally arrived from Raith Rovers on a development loan the previous summer. The Kirkcaldy-born defender was handed his first-team debut by Pedro Caixinha for the Scottish Premiership clash with Kilmarnock at Rugby Park in April. The 6ft 4" stopper began his career at his home town club Raith Rovers, where he was loaned out to East Stirling in the first part of 2015. He caught the eye when he broke through at Raith in the Championship before moving on loan to Brechin City. Rangers' attention was brought to Bates when he returned to Raith, making nine top team starts, including in a 1-0 defeat to the Ibrox side at Stark's Park.

## ROSS McCRORIE

The Scotland youth international is another youngster for whom the club has high hopes. He spent the latter half of last season on loan at Dumbarton, his experience with the Sons an important factor in his career development. The teenage defender is looking to continue his footballing education alongside the likes of the vastly experienced Bruno Alves as he prepares to keep pushing for first-team opportunities.

## LEE HODSON

The Northern Ireland international put pen to paper on a three year deal after returning from his country's European Championship campaign in France, his arrival bringing added competition at full back. The former Watford, Brentford and MK Dons defender spent the second half of his first season on loan with Kilmarnock. He made 17 appearances in total for Killie, including two against the Light Blues. Having been part of Northern Ireland's squad in France, Hodson enjoyed a short break before joining up with the Rangers squad.

## JAMES TAVERNIER

Rangers signed James Tavernier on a three year deal from English League One club Wigan in July 2015 and, such was his impact at Ibrox, he soon signed a 12 month contract extension. Born in Bradford, he started his career with Leeds United as an academy player and he spent seven years at Elland Road before he joined Newcastle United in 2008. He signed pro with the Premier League club in 2009 and, despite being a Magpies player until 2014, he only ever made two appearances for the first-team. Newcastle chose to loan him out to six clubs during his time on Tyneside – Gateshead, Carlisle, Sheffield Wednesday, Milton Keynes Dons, Shrewsbury Town and Rotherham United. At Rotherham he enjoyed his first major success as a senior player, making 27 appearances, scoring five goals and helping them to promotion to the Championship via the play-offs in the 2013/14 season.

## AIDAN WILSON

The youngster was delighted to sign an extension to his contract in May, the new agreement keeping him at Ibrox until the summer of 2019. The highly-rated defender, who comes from Helensburgh, made his top-team debut against Aberdeen at Ibrox towards the end of last season. With his future secured for the time being, he will be hoping to continue to impress as he targets more chances in the Light Blues first-team.

## DANIEL CANDEIAS

Winger Daniel Candeias signed a two year deal after leaving Benfica, the wide man being reunited with Pedro Caixinha after the pair worked together at Nacional during the 2011/12 season. Candeias started his senior career with Porto, where he made four first-team appearances before a string of loans sent him to Portuguese sides Varzim, Rio Ave and Paços de Ferreira as well as Spanish side Recreativo. It was in his next permanent move that Candeias first met Caixinha when he signed for Nacional, making 85 appearances over four years and scoring 13 goals. Candeias moved to Benfica in 2014 but never made an appearance for the club, instead he has enjoyed loan moves to FC Nürnberg in Germany, scoring two, in 16 appearances; Granada CF in Spain where he played 11 times and FC Metz in France, netting two in 28 games. He made 30 appearances on loan for Turks Alanyaspor during the 2016/17 season, scoring four goals. Candeias represented Portugal from Under-16 to Under-23 level, scoring 22 goals at youth level for his country.

## JASON HOLT

Rangers are set to enjoy the best of Jason Holt, with the midfielder contracted to the club until 2020. Rangers' fans will remember the diminutive midfielder for his impressive strike against Gers in Hearts' 2-0 victory at Tynecastle in November 2014. That was one of two goals he netted for Hearts during the 2014/15 campaign before he moved to Sheffield United in January 2015 for the remainder of the season. Holt made 11 starts for the League One side and scored five goals. That wasn't his first loan away from Tynecastle; Holt also had a spell with Raith Rovers during the 2011/12 season – he made five appearances for the Fife side and scored once in his time at Stark's Park. Born and bred in Edinburgh, Holt had been at Hearts since he was nine, having risen through their youth system to progress to the first-team. He played his boys football for Musselburgh Windsor before joining Hearts in 2002. He went on to turn out for the Capital side 62 times and scored seven goals, two of those coming against Celtic.

## JORDAN ROSSITER

Highly-rated midfielder Jordan Rossiter signed a four year deal at Ibrox in May 2016 to leave Liverpool, the club he had been at since a boy. The England youth had been courted by a number of top clubs before electing to join the Gers and the Light Blues fans will be hoping to see him realise his full potential at Ibrox after an injury-hit season last term. Rossiter made five first-team appearances for his boyhood club after captaining and graduating from the Liverpool academy, including featuring against Sion in the Europa League, Jürgen Klopp's first game in charge of the Merseyside club. He also scored his only goal for the Reds to open the scoring in stunning style against Middlesbrough, in a League Cup tie which saw Liverpool win 14-13 on penalties.

# Player Profiles

## JOSH WINDASS

The son of former Aberdeen striker Dean Windass, Josh was secured on a pre-contract in January 2016 alongside his Accrington Stanley teammate Matt Crooks. The pair signed agreements with Rangers in the New Year which saw them join up with Mark Warburton's side in the summer. The pacey midfielder began his career at Huddersfield Town before a leg break forced him to give up the game for a short period, working as a labourer. He began playing non-league football for Harrogate Railway Athletic before Accrington Stanley made a move for him. Windass spent three years at Stanley, making 75 appearances and scoring 23 goals. He scored 17 goals in his final season there before moving to Ibrox, where he scored on his debut whilst the Gers toured America.

## RYAN JACK

The former Aberdeen captain made 250 appearances for the Dons after coming through their youth system, making his first-team debut in a League Cup clash against Raith Rovers in September 2010. A Scotland youth international from Under-16 level through to the Under-21s, he was a member of the Aberdeen team which won the League Cup in 2014 with a penalty shoot-out victory over Inverness Caledonian Thistle at Celtic Park. At the start of the 2015/16 campaign, and at the age of just 23, he was then named as the club's new skipper following Russell Anderson's retirement. He moved to Ibrox on a free transfer following the end of his contract at Pittodrie, signing a three year deal with Rangers.

## CARLOS PEÑA

The Mexican international signed a three year deal with Rangers in the summer. Known as 'Gullit' in his homeland because of his similarity to Dutch legend Ruud, 27 year old Peña joined the Light Blues from Liga MX side Guadalajara. Capped 19 times by his country and selected for the 2014 World Cup, the attacking midfielder broke new ground with his move to Glasgow as he hadn't previously played for a club outside of Mexico, having had spells with Pachuca, Leon and Guadalajara, who paid a reported £8 million for the playmaker in December 2015. Peña returned to Leon on loan in December 2016 and will now get an opportunity to show Rangers fans what he can do. A skilful, creative player in the middle of the park, Peña can break up attacks and push forward with a desire to provide assists or find the net himself.

## NIKO KRANJČAR

With a top-level career spanning 15 years, the vastly experienced Croatian was been another valuable addition to the squad, although a knee ligament injury ruled him out for most of last season. Born in Zagreb, he started his senior professional career at Dinamo Zagreb, becoming the club's youngest captain at 17. Portsmouth gave him his first taste of English football at 22, with Harry Redknapp paying £5 million in August 2006 for one of football's rising stars. Prior to this switch, the young Croat was handed an international debut against Israel by his father Zlatko and he would go on to make 81 appearances for his country, scoring 16 goals. In nine years – from 2004 to 2013 – he would represent Croatia at the 2006 World Cup, Euro 2008 and Euro 2012. The 2008 FA Cup winner with Portsmouth became the third Croatian to play for Rangers – following in the footsteps of Dado Pršo and Nikica Jelavić.

# JORDAN THOMPSON

After spending four years on the books at Manchester United, Thompson moved to Ibrox in the summer of 2015 after a successful trial with the Light Blues. The Northern Irishman made his top-team debut against Alloa Athletic in November 2015. He then subsequently spent a brief time on loan at Airdrieonians and then Raith Rovers, where he earned very positive reviews following his performances for the Kirkcaldy side.

# JAMIE BARJONAS

A midfielder, he joined the Rangers Academy when at primary school and has matured through the various age groups. His big moment came when he made his debut for the club in May 2017. He came off the bench to help his team record a 2-1 victory over Partick Thistle at Firhill.

# RYAN HARDIE

The front man made his professional debut for the club in the 2014/15 League Cup when he came off the bench against Falkirk as the Light Blues recorded a 3-1 victory. He marked his first start for Rangers in the best possible fashion, netting two goals in an away game against Dumbarton in April 2015. The boyhood Rangers fan has represented Scotland at various age levels.

# DÁLCIO

The attacker is at Ibrox on a season-long loan from Benfica in Portugal. He joined Benfica from Belenenses in 2015 before having a spell back there on loan, where he gained experience in the Europa League, playing against Lech Poznań and Fiorentina. He has represented Portugal at Under-19 and Under-20 level and last season spent the bulk of his time with Benfica's 'B' team, making 33 appearances and scoring three times.

# KENNY MILLER

The striker continues to prove age is no barrier to scoring goals - Miller is enjoying his third spell at the club and is as potent as ever in the penalty box. He became one of only five post-war players to play for both Old Firm clubs when he signed for Celtic in 2006. He spent only a season at Parkhead before signing for Derby County for a year. Kenny returned north of the border for a hugely successful period between 2008 and 2011. He won three top-flight league titles, the Scottish Cup and the League Cup during Walter Smith's reign. The front man made his Scotland debut in 2001, in a friendly against Poland, and he scored his first international goal against Iceland in March 2003. The prolific forward went on to make 68 appearances for his country, netting 18 goals.

# Player Profiles

## DECLAN JOHN

The Welsh international arrived on a year-long loan on the last day of this summer's transfer window. The 22-year-old brings plenty of experience, having played for Cardiff City in the English Premier League and Championship. The Ibrox club's tenth first-team signing of the summer, he has represented his country from youth right through to full international level. A left-back by trade, John has also featured at left wing-back on occasion, and is in the final year of his contract at Cardiff having signed a five-year deal in 2013. He made his full Wales debut in October 2013, with the Dragons defeating Macedonia 1-0 in a World Cup qualifier in Cardiff.

## ALFREDO MORELOS

The striker created a little bit of Rangers history when he became the first Colombian to sign for the Light Blues in the summer, penning a three year contract at Ibrox. He arrived from HJK Helsinki in Finland. The young striker is a Colombian international at Under-20 level and began his career at Independiente Medellín in his homeland before moving to HJK, initially on loan, before his move was made permanent at the start of 2017. His season on loan in the Finnish capital was impressive as he netted 30 goals in 43 games, with four of them coming in the Europa League qualifying round.

## GRAHAM DORRANS

The midfielder completed a move from Norwich to Rangers for an undisclosed fee after signing a three year deal with the Light Blues in July 2017. He became the ninth new recruit of the summer for Pedro Caixinha and joined the club he grew up supporting after spending nine years in England. He started his career with Livingston and, after a loan spell at Partick Thistle, joined West Bromwich Albion in 2008 before moving to Norwich in 2015. He has vast experience of the Premier League with both clubs and has goals against the likes of Arsenal and Manchester City to his name. Capped by Scotland 12 times, the 30 year old followed the signings of Bruno Alves, Ryan Jack, Dálcio, Fábio Cardoso, Daniel Candeias, Alfredo Morelos, Eduardo Herrera and Carlos Peña. At international level, he also played at the 2006 UEFA Under-19 Championships, as Scotland made it all the way to the final with Dorrans scoring in the 2-1 final defeat to Spain, before going on to represent his nation the following summer at the Under-20 World Cup.

## EDUARDO HERRERA

Mexico international Eduardo Herrera signed a three year deal in the summer of 2017, the 28 year old striker joining from Pumas in his homeland. He had been at the Liga MX side since 2007, making 186 appearances and scoring 56 times. He played there for six years before being loaned to Santos Laguna where he first joined up with Pedro Caixinha. At 6ft 2in Herrera is a towering forward and he netted five times in 21 appearances during the 2013/14 season under the Portuguese manager. More recently he has been on loan at Veracruz, scoring three in eight. He scored 57 goals in 207 appearances in Mexico. Herrera was capped for the first time by Mexico in March 2015 and scored his first international goal in a friendly against Paraguay.

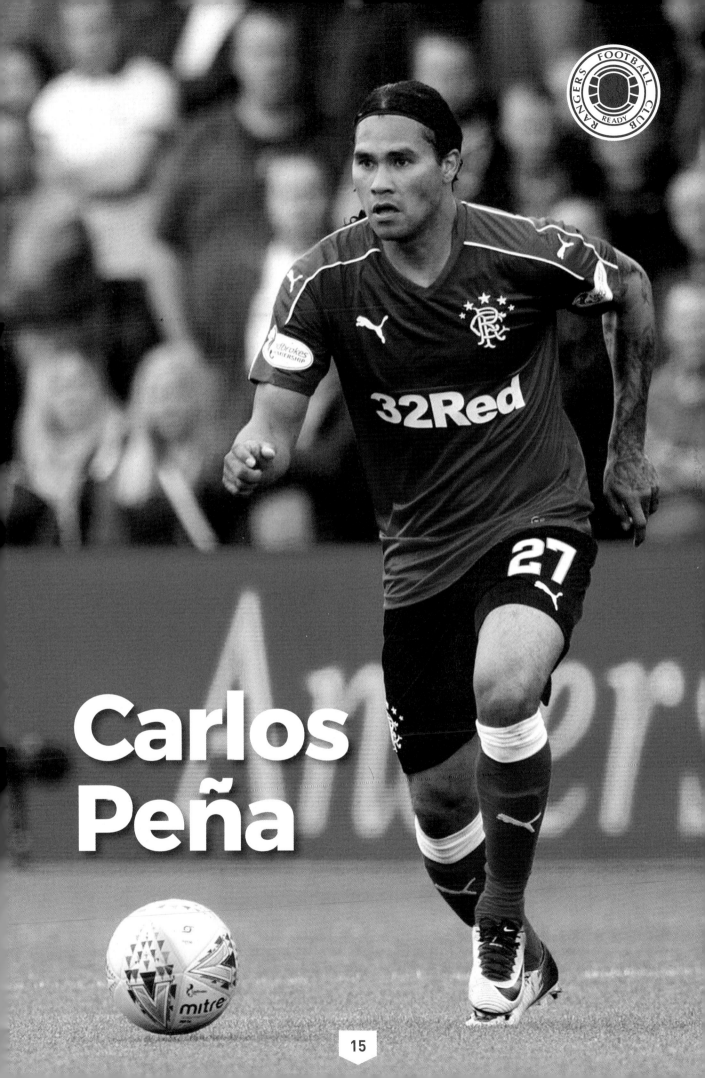

# Carlos Peña

# Wordsearch

Find the words in the grid. Words can go horizontally, vertically and diagonally in all eight directions.

| | | | | | | | | | |
|---|---|---|---|---|---|---|---|---|---|
| R | X | N | N | H | T | U | R | T | S |
| G | M | C | C | O | I | S | T | M | B |
| A | Q | D | R | R | W | Z | K | P | K |
| S | S | W | D | E | G | T | B | L | L |
| C | S | A | R | T | G | O | M | A | R |
| O | E | D | H | X | G | V | U | E | H |
| I | N | D | P | A | C | D | P | G | D |
| G | U | E | L | B | R | O | W | X | H |
| N | O | L | Z | U | O | P | B | V | Q |
| E | S | L | P | C | S | M | I | T | H |

Baxter        McCoist
Cooper        Smith
Gascoigne     Souness
Gough         Struth
Laudrup       Waddell

Answer on page 60

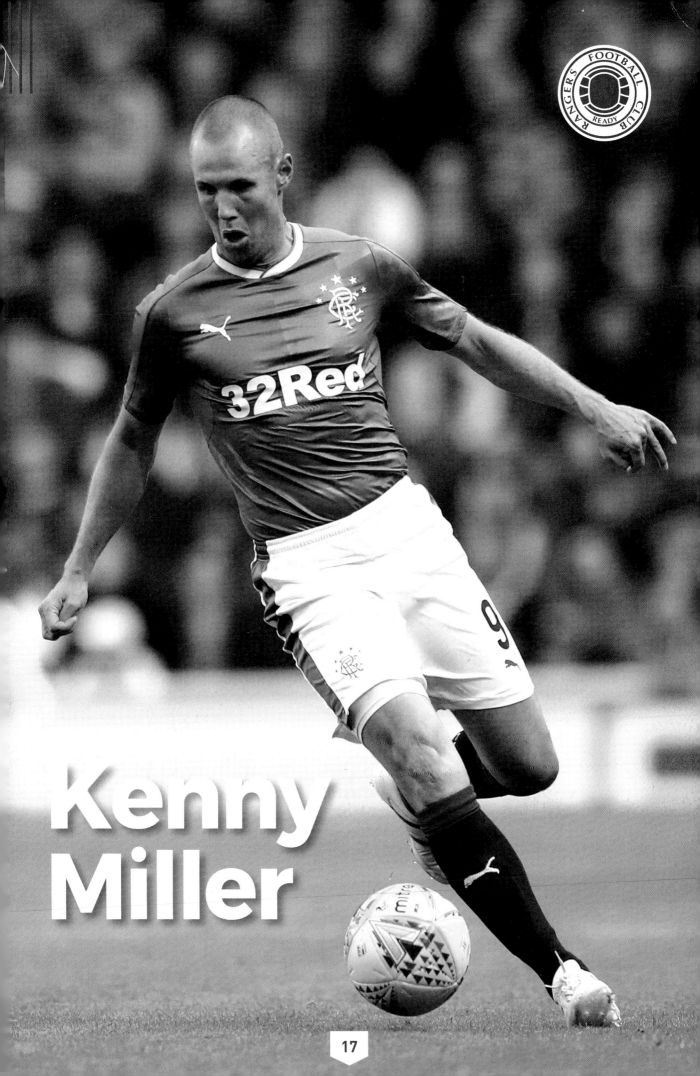

# Kenny Miller

# Jack The Glad

As he kicked a ball about his school playground and local park, or watched games on television, Ryan Jack no doubt allowed himself a moment or two to dream of the day he might pull on the famous Rangers jersey.

A boyhood Gers supporter, there could be nothing better than imagining himself striding out in front of a packed Ibrox Stadium to meet the acclaim of thousands of appreciative fans.

Much to his delight, that dream became a reality when Pedro Caixinha made the midfielder his first Scottish signing in the summer, Jack following Bruno Alves through the Ibrox entrance.

Having watched him in action as captain of Premiership rivals Aberdeen, the new Ibrox boss quickly pinpointed Jack as one of the players he wanted to be a cornerstone of his rebuilding plans.

When the Glasgow giants came calling, there was only going to be one answer from the player who had spent the previous three seasons at Pittodrie.

"I was a Rangers fan growing up, my mum's side were all Rangers fans," he said.

"I think it sunk in when I went into Ibrox with my family. I had my missus and my daughter with me and we all had a look around.

"Standing in the tunnel it really hit home that I was a Rangers player.

"I'm delighted to be here and it's an honour to be part of this club."

Jack, who counts Rangers legend Paul Gascoigne as one of his heroes, has penned a three-year deal with the Light Blues. As a Dons player, he was always impressed by the atmosphere created by the home fans at Ibrox and he's looking forward to performing for the Govan faithful for the foreseeable future.

RYAN JACK

"I've mentioned before to friends and family that the 2-1 game when Rangers beat Aberdeen at Ibrox, the atmosphere that I experienced that day was probably the best I have experienced in my career", he said.

"Obviously I was on the losing side that day and it was a difficult one to take, but it's atmospheres like that, and the European nights under the lights, that you want to play in.

"It's an honour and a privilege to come to such a massive club and to have this opportunity.

"I've had a lot of experiences as a football player and to captain Aberdeen Football Club was a huge honour.

"I'm thankful to Aberdeen for that and to Derek McInnes but I just felt it was time for a fresh challenge.

"I'm here, I want to enjoy it and I want to help the club be successful again."

His manager was delighted to secure his signature, Caixinha saying, "I believe 25 is a great age for him to come here.

"He had three years as captain of Aberdeen and has that experience, and he understands what it means to represent Rangers."

INTERVIEW

# Season Review
## 2016/17

## European Reunion

Last season saw Rangers book a return ticket to European football, much to the delight of their thousands of supporters and everyone associated with the club. Here we take a look back at some of the highlights of the Premiership campaign and some of the key results which helped secure qualification for the Europa League.

### Saturday 6th August, 2016

### Rangers 1 – 1 Hamilton

It was a day filled with excitement and expectation but Rangers' first match back in the Scottish Premiership didn't quite have the ending the fans were hoping for, with the home side having to settle for a share of the spoils with Hamilton Accies at Ibrox Stadium.

Trailing by an Ali Crawford goal to nil at the interval, Martyn Waghorn equalised in the second half but the Light Blues couldn't find a winner in the closing stages.

With 50,000 supporters crammed into Ibrox, chairman Dave King was given a warm welcome by the home support prior to kick-off as he unfurled the Championship flag to officially confirm the club's return to the top flight.

**GOAL:** Waghorn

**RANGERS:** Foderingham, Tavernier, Kiernan, Hill, Wallace; Barton, Halliday (Rossiter, 76), Kranjčar (Forrester, 60), McKay, Miller (O'Halloran, 60), Waghorn.

**SUBS NOT USED:** Gilks, Hodson, Holt, Dodoo.

## Saturday 13th August, 2016
### Dundee 1 – 2 Rangers

Another little piece of history was made at Dens Park as Rangers recorded their first Scottish Premiership win in four years after a hard-fought win over hosts Dundee.

After what was, at times, a highly impressive first-half from the visitors, the second half was less so, but they held out for an oh-so-important and deserved victory.

The opening to the game was scrappy to say the least, with both sides struggling to put any period of passing together, although Rangers soon got their act in gear with their regular game flowing on the lush Dundonian turf.

## Saturday 20th August, 2016
### Rangers 2 - 1 Motherwell

Kenny Miller was the Rangers hero as his stunning last-minute strike secured all three points on a memorable afternoon at Ibrox.

With the scoreline sitting at 1-1 after Motherwell's Scott McDonald and Harry Forrester had found the net on 19 and 63 minutes respectively, the Light Blues needed a moment of magic and they got it once again from that man Miller.

Niko Kranjčar cross was skewed wide by Michael O'Halloran but it fell perfectly for Rangers' No. 9, who guided an accurate shot beyond Craig Samson to send the home supporters wild with delight.

**GOALS:** Forrester, Miller

**RANGERS:** Foderingham; Tavernier, Kiernan, Wilson, Wallace; Rossiter, Barton, Halliday (Kranjčar, 62); Forrester (O'Halloran, 67), Miller (Dodoo, 62), McKay.

**SUBS NOT USED:**
Gilks, Hill, Hodson, Bates.

**GOALS:** Forrester, Miller

**RANGERS:** Foderingham; Tavernier, Kiernan, Wilson, Wallace; Barton, Rossiter, Halliday (Kranjčar 56); McKay (Dodoo, 56), Miller, Forrester (O'Halloran, 66).

**SUBS NOT USED:**
Gilks, Hill, Hodson, Bates, O'Halloran.

# Season Review
## 2016/17

### Saturday 1st October, 2016
### Rangers 2 - 0 Partick Thistle

Rangers returned to winning ways in the Scottish Premiership with a hard-fought victory over Partick Thistle at Ibrox Stadium.

In what was something of a derby match, the biggest home crowd of the season so far – 49,680 – rocked up in Govan to see goals from Niko Kranjčar and Andy Halliday ensure the three points remained on the south side of the Clyde.

It had been a frustrating few weeks for the Light Blues but the well deserved win sent the team into the international break in a much better frame of mind.

**GOALS:** Kranjčar, Halliday

**RANGERS:** Foderingham; Tavernier, Senderos, Wilson, Wallace; Halliday, Holt, Kranjčar (Forrester, 74); Waghorn (Garner, 62), Miller, McKay (Dodoo, 62).

**SUBS NOT USED:**
Gilks, Hodson, O'Halloran, Crooks, Kiernan.

### Friday 14th October, 2016
### Inverness CT 0 - 1 Rangers

Striker supreme Kenny Miller became only the 16th post war player to score 100 goals for Rangers as his strike proved the difference between the two sides in Inverness.

The striker's beautifully taken volley won the game for the Gers and took all three points away from the trip to the Highlands to give his side a crucial away win.

It was a testing night for the Light Blues who had to work hard for their victory, with Inverness providing a nervy end to the encounter.

**GOAL:** Miller

**RANGERS:** Foderingham, Tavernier, Hill, Kiernan, Wallace, Halliday, Holt, Kranjčar (Windass, 74'), McKay (Garner, 69'), Miller, Waghorn (Dodoo, 69').

**SUBS NOT USED:**
Gilks, Forrester, Hodson, Senderos.

# Saturday 29th October, 2016
## Rangers 3 - 0 Kilmarnock

Remembrance Day at Ibrox proved to be a memorable day for Rangers fans at a sold out Ibrox with their side strolling to an impressive win over Kilmarnock.

An L118 light gun was fired by soldiers from 207 (City of Glasgow) Battery, part of 105 Regiment Royal Artlillery, at the start and end of a perfectly observed minute of silence before kick-off.

Rangers, wearing commemorative poppy shirts, looked the part as they claimed all three points in front of a huge crowd of 49,302.

A terrific goal from Lee Wallace after 15 minutes was just what the doctor ordered after the frustrating midweek draw with St Johnstone. Andy Halliday tucked away a penalty before the half-hour mark to make it 2-0. Joe Garner added a third just after the break and, given the number of chances Rangers created, the only surprise was that they failed to extend their lead further.

**GOALS:** Wallace, Halliday (pen), Garner

**RANGERS:** Foderingham; Tavernier, Kiernan, Hill, Wallace; Windass (Crooks, 75), Halliday, Holt; O'Halloran, Garner (Dodoo,70), Miller (Waghorn, 70).

**SUBS NOT USED:** Gilks, McKay, Forrester, Hodson.

# Season Review
## 2016/17

### Saturday 19th November, 2016
#### Rangers 1 – 0 Dundee

Super sub Harry Forrester recreated his incredible form against Dundee as he rescued all three points for the Gers with a superb header in stoppage time.

A second-half replacement, he scored his third goal in three games against the Dees after the Gers looked like they would have to settle for a draw.

Despite laying siege to the visitors' goal after the break, Rangers couldn't find the clinical edge until Forrester popped up in the 93rd minute to guide a glancing header, with his back to goal, in at the far post.

**GOAL:** Forrester

**RANGERS:** Foderingham, Tavernier, Hill, Kiernan, Wallace; Halliday, Holt, Windass (McKay, 65'); O'Halloran (Dodoo, 71'), Garner, Miller (Forrester 76').

**SUBS NOT USED:** Gilks, Wilson, Hodson, Crooks.

### Saturday 26th November, 2016
#### Partick Thistle 1 - 2 Rangers

For the second week running Rangers snatched a win in the last minute of the game as substitute Joe Dodoo proved the difference in Glasgow's West End.

It was an end-to-end affair and culminated in a thrilling finale at Firhill. Both sides had plenty of chances but it took until the 75th minute for Kris Doolan to open the scoring for Thistle. Dodoo cancelled that out within five minutes with a wonderful strike.

The summer signing's brace was rounded off in the 94th minute of the match; a perfect finish to end an entertaining afternoon of football which sent the Light Blue second in the table.

**GOALS:** Dodoo (2)

**RANGERS:** Foderingham, Tavernier, Wilson, Kiernan, Wallace; Halliday, Holt, Windass (McKay, 45'); Miller, Garner (Dodoo, 60'), Forrester (O'Halloran, 74').

**SUBS NOT USED:** Gilks, Hodson, Senderos, Waghorn.

## Saturday 3rd December, 2016

### Rangers 2 - 1 Aberdeen

An excellent display of grit, determination and some tremendous football saw Rangers return to winning ways with victory over Aberdeen.

In what was a terrific game of football, with chances at both ends and plenty of blood and thunder, goals from Kenny Miller and Lee Hodson – his first in light blue – saw Gers provide the perfect tonic to their midweek reverse to Hearts at Tynecastle.

The final minute of normal time then saw Clint Hill sent off for a second bookable offence after a tug on James Maddison in midfield, and then a mass flare-up in injury time saw Dons skipper Ryan Jack dismissed.

Andrew Considine then netted a consolation deep in stoppage time but it couldn't take the gloss off a hugely satisfying afternoon for the home fans who again turned out in their droves to record the first 50,000-plus crowd of the season.

**GOALS:** Miller, Hodson

**RANGERS:** Foderingham; Hodson, Kiernan, Hill, Wallace; Halliday, Holt, Miller (Tavernier, 64); O'Halloran (Waghorn, 66), Garner, McKay (Forrester, 77).

**SUBS NOT USED:** Gilks, Wilson, Dodoo, Crooks.

## Saturday 10th December 10, 2016

### Rangers 2 - 0 Hearts

Rangers didn't have to wait long to exact revenge on their Edinburgh rivals with a dominant display from start to finish.

Goals either side of half-time saw the Gers stay in second in the Premiership. Rob Kiernan netted his first competitive goal for the club with a superb header on 29 minutes, before Barrie McKay dinked home just after the break.

Ian Cathro was taking charge of the Jambos for the first time but couldn't engineer a win as Rangers limited Hearts to very few openings in front of the goal.

**GOALS:** Kiernan, McKay

**RANGERS:** Foderingham, Hodson, Kiernan, Wilson, Wallace; Halliday, Holt, Tav; McKay (Burt, 90'), Garner (Dodoo, 88'), Miller (Waghorn, 60').

**SUBS NOT USED:** Gilks, Senderos, Crooks, O'Halloran.

# Season Review

2016/17

## Friday 16th December, 2016

### Hamilton 1 - 2 Rangers

A Martyn Waghorn double was enough to see off Hamilton Accies on a chill Lanarkshire evening at New Douglas Park.

Rangers were utterly dominant for long spells of the match and ought to have won by a wider margin, and indeed they were made to sweat late on as Dougie Imrie pulled one back for Martin Canning's men.

Despite that, Gers held on to record their third league win in succession for the first time this season in what was proving to be a very successful month.

**GOALS:** Waghorn (2)

**RANGERS:** Foderingham; Hodson, Kiernan, Wilson, Wallace; Tavernier, Halliday, Holt; Waghorn (Forrester, 76), Garner, McKay.

**SUBS NOT USED:**
Gilks, Dodoo, Miller, Senderos, O'Halloran, Hill.

## Saturday 24th December, 2016

### Rangers 1 - 0 Inverness Caledonian Thistle

Rangers made it four wins on the bounce with a hard-fought victory over Inverness at Ibrox Stadium to send their supporters home full of festive cheer.

A Brad McKay own-goal after 13 minutes was the difference between the two sides in this Christmas Eve match, but it was a scrappy affair with Gers creating little in the way of goal-scoring opportunities.

The performance was secondary however, with another maximum points haul being all that mattered to the Govan faithful.

**GOAL:** McKay (og)

**RANGERS:** Foderingham; Hodson, Kiernan, Hill, Wallace; Tavernier (Windass, 59), Holt, Halliday; Waghorn (Forrester, 72), Garner, McKay (Miller, 59).

**SUBS NOT USED:**
Gilks, Wilson, Dodoo, O'Halloran.

## Saturday 28th January, 2017
## Motherwell 0 - 2 Rangers

Motherwell must be sick of the sight of Kenny Miller as the striker proved to be the difference between the sides for the second time in seven days after his Scottish Cup exploits.

The veteran striker popped up 18 minutes from time to poke the ball over the line at Fir Park and help put Rangers back into second spot in the Premiership. Emerson Hyndman shone on his first start for the Light Blues and the 20 year old topped it off with a well-taken goal on 87 minutes to make sure of the three points for the Gers.

It was an eventful afternoon which saw Rangers down to 10 men after just four minutes when Michael O'Halloran was shown red for a rash, high challenge. But the Steelmen had to compete for most of the game too; missing a man when Scott McDonald got his marching orders for a tackle on goalscorer Miller after 26 minutes.

**GOALS:** Miller, Hyndman

**RANGERS:** Foderingham, Tavernier, Kiernan, Hill, Wallace, Halliday, Toral (Waghorn, 68'), Hyndman, McKay (Forrester, 76'), Miller (Windass, 80'), O'Halloran.

**SUBS NOT USED:** Gilks, Senderos, Holt, Dodoo.

**GOALS:** McKay, Waghorn, Hyndman

**RANGERS:** Foderingham; Tavernier, Kiernan, Hill, Wallace; Holt, Toral (Halliday, 82), Hyndman; Waghorn (Wilson, 82), Miller (Garner, 64), McKay.

**SUBS NOT USED:** Alnwick, Forrester, Hodson, O'Halloran.

## Wednesday 1st March 1, 2017
## Rangers 3 - 2 St Johnstone

After a month to forget, Emerson Hyndman scored an injury-time winner for 10-man Rangers to sink St Johnstone in a dramatic match at Ibrox Stadium.

Leading 2-0 through Barrie McKay and Martyn Waghorn, David Wotherspoon pulled one back for Saints before Rob Kiernan was sent off and Steven Anderson levelled matters

But, as Gers looked to be heading to a fifth league match without victory, Hyndman struck to send Ibrox wild with delight.

# Season Review
## 2016/17

### Celtic 1 - 1 Rangers

Rangers fought back from a goal down to earn a deserved point at Celtic Park this afternoon in the Old Firm derby.

Despite their good play and possession, the visitors fell behind on the 35 minute mark. On the edge of his own box, Jason Holt stumbled on the rutted Parkhead surface with the ball falling to James Forrest. He fed Stuart Armstrong who rifled a 20-yard drive beyond the reach of Foderingham and into the back of the net.

The second half saw Rangers dominate proceedings. They scored a deserved equaliser with two minutes of normal time remaining when Clint Hill latched onto a rebound at the back post to sweep the ball home to spark quite extraordinary scenes of celebration in the Rangers end.

The result was a huge confidence booster for Rangers who could now enter the Pedro Caixinha era full of optimism.

**GOAL:** Hill

**RANGERS:** Foderingham; Hodson, Hill, Wilson, Wallace; Tavernier, Holt, Hyndman, McKay (Windass, 59); Waghorn (O'Halloran, 84), Miller.

**SUBS NOT USED:**
Alnwick, Dodoo, Senderos, Bates.

## Saturday 18th March, 2017

### Rangers 4 - 0 Hamilton

The Pedro Caixinha era at Rangers got off to a dream start as the Light Blues recorded their biggest Premiership win of the season – crushing Hamilton Academical 4-0 at Ibrox Stadium.

Goals from Emerson Hyndman and Clint Hill in the first half and Martyn Waghorn and Lee Wallace in the second made it a comfortable first day at the office for the Portuguese manager.

In front of a capacity home crowd, section BF1 unfurled a banner prior to kick-off welcoming the new boss, and thanking interim gaffer Graeme Murty for his efforts over the last month.

**GOALS:** Hyndman, Hill, Waghorn, Wallace

**RANGERS:** Foderingham; Tavernier, Wilson, Hill, Wallace; Hyndman, Toral, Holt, McKay (Garner, 66); Miller; Waghorn (Dodoo, 76).

**SUBS NOT USED:**
Alnwick, Hodson, Senderos, Windass.

## Sunday 9th April, 2017
### Aberdeen 0 - 3 Rangers

The visitors produced a stunning three goals in four minutes to defeat Aberdeen at Pittodrie for the first time in over six years.

Having been up against it for much of the second half, Kenny Miller bagged an incredible brace before substitute Joe Dodoo rounded off the rout to send the thousands of travelling Gers supporters back to Glasgow in raptures.

The outcome had looked unlikely as the match drew to a close but Miller broke the deadlock in the 79th minute before doubling his side's advantage just two minutes later. With the Dons on the ropes, Dodoo completed the stunning victory with his side's third with 83 minutes on the clock.

**GOALS:** Miller (2), Dodoo

**RANGERS:** Foderingham, Tavernier, Bates, D. Wilson, Beerman, Holt, Hyndman (Windass, 53), Toral, Miller, Garner (Dodoo, 70), Waghorn (Halliday, 80).

**SUBS NOT USED:**
Alnwick, McKay, Hodson, A. Wilson.

## Saturday 15th April, 2017
### Rangers 2 - 0 Partick Thistle

Rangers won the Glasgow derby at Ibrox Stadium, deservedly seeing off Alan Archibald's Partick Thistle.

Kenny Miller netted the opener six minutes before the interval with Jon Toral adding a second with 54 minutes on the clock.

The Light Blues remained unbeaten under new boss Pedro Caixinha after five games, with the most impressive stat from his time in charge being the concession of just one goal.

**GOALS:** Miller, Toral

**RANGERS:** Foderingham, Tavernier, Bates, Wilson, Beerman, Holt, Hyndman, Toral (Halliday, 84), Miller, Waghorn (Garner, 75), McKay (Dodoo, 45).

**SUBS NOT USED:**
Alnwick, Windass, Hodson, Wilson.

# Season Review

## 2016/17

### Sunday 7th May, 2017

### Partick Thistle 1 - 2 Rangers

Joe Garner headed a 94th minute winner as Rangers came from behind to defeat Partick Thistle and guarantee their place in the Europa League.

Trailing 1-0 to an early Chris Doolan strike, substitute Barrie McKay scored with eight minutes left before Garner won the game in injury time in an almost carbon copy of Gers' last visit to Firhill in November, where Joe Dodoo struck right at the end to secure a comeback 2-1 win.

It sparked wild celebrations in the packed Rangers end and provided everyone with a much-needed boost after a tough few weeks with smiling fans heading home to start looking out for their passports once again.

**GOALS:** McKay, Garner

**RANGERS:** Foderingham; Tavernier, Bates, Wilson (Barjonas, 66), Beerman; Holt (McKay, 75), Windass; Waghorn (Hill, 53), Miller, Dodoo; Garner.

**SUBS NOT USED:**
Alnwick, Halliday, Atakayi, Dallas.

### Saturday 13th May, 2017

### Rangers 2 - 1 Hearts

It may have been mission accomplished seven days previously as far as Europe was concerned, but there was no let-up from Pedro Caixinha's men as they swept Hearts aside at Ibrox.

It was the same scoreline and the same scorers as their last-gasp win over Partick Thistle but Rangers' win was a lot more straightforward against the Jambos, who were reduced to 10 men in the first half with the dismissal of midfielder Prince Buaben.

Joe Garner and Barrie McKay netted in each half and on either side of an Esmael Goncalves equaliser, which came against the run of play.

**GOALS:** Garner, McKay

**RANGERS:** Foderingham, Tavernier, Hill, Bates, Hodson, Holt (Barjonas, 66'), Toral (Waghorn, 73'), Windass (Dodoo, 52'), McKay, Miller, Garner.

**SUBS NOT USED:**
Alnwick, Beerman, A. Wilson, Halliday.

# Sunday 21st May, 2017
## St Johnstone 1 - 2 Rangers

Rangers brought the curtain down on the campaign with another victory, this time over St Johnstone in Perth.

After a muted opening, Rangers turned the screw on the Saints and dominated proceedings at McDiarmid Park, Kenny Miller firing his side ahead five minutes before half-time.

Before that the Gers had offered little in front of goal while St Johnstone had gone close on a number of occasions.

But it was a different story in the second-half with Jon Toral signing off his Rangers career with a well taken third goal for the club.

**GOALS:** Miller, Toral

**RANGERS:** Alnwick, Tavernier, A. Wilson, Bates, Beerman, Holt, Barjonas (Halliday, 89'), Toral (McKay, 75'), Windass, Waghorn (Bradley, 84'), Miller.

**SUBS NOT USED:** Foderingham, Dodoo, Lyon, Atakayi.

# Winning Feeling

## Bruno's vow to bring the good times back to Ibrox

The first signing of Pedro Caixinha's rebuilding project at Ibrox, fellow-Portuguese Bruno Alves knows a thing or two about what it takes to be a winner in football.

The gifted defender has amassed an impressive haul of medals during a glittering career, the pinnacle of which was reached when helping his country win the 2016 European Championships in France.

He made just one appearance in the finals, an impressive performance as Wales were beaten 2-0 in the semi-finals.

His magnificent international achievements aside – his near-100 cap tally since his debut in 2007 covering Olympics and World Cups as well as the Euros success – wherever the centre-half has gone, silverware has generally followed.

Alves won four successive league titles in his homeland with Porto. A big-money move to Russia saw him win the championship on two occasions with Zenit St Petersburg before repeating the feat with Turkish side Fenerbahçe in 2013-14.

Add to that a clutch of domestic cups with all three clubs and it's apparent Rangers' first signing of the summer is something special.

Despite his medal-laden career, he is hungry for more success and has made it clear that is the reason why he chose to sign a two-year deal at Ibrox after leaving Serie A outfit Cagliari.

"I have this feeling and this desire to win and I think to move here will bring this back to me and to my career," he said.

"At almost all the clubs I have played for, I win. And I expect to win here for the fans and for the club – I think I can do this here."

BRUNO ALVE

It is has been a number of years since Rangers were last crowned champions of Scotland, but Alves is focused on setting that record straight during his stay in Glasgow.

He said: "I will do my best to win. That's the main reason why I come here.

"I want to be a champion again.

"This is one of the best feelings that I have in my career and the last time I was a champion at a club was in Fenerbahçe. I want to have this feeling again.

"I think I come here for the right reasons and I think that I can bring this back to the club.

"It's going to be an amazing journey, I'm sure about that."

The stopper is no stranger to his new home, having been on Champions League duty at Ibrox with Porto in September 2005.

He didn't play in the group stage match which Alex McLeish's Rangers won 3-2 but recalls the Glasgow tie particularly well.

"For me it was a very good experience and this also made me come here, to receive the affection and the support of the fans," he said.

"All the people that come here, they will never forget about what they see and what they experienced. It's a fantastic environment."

# Guess Who?

We've mixed up a few Rangers players to make some interesting faces! Can you work out who's who?

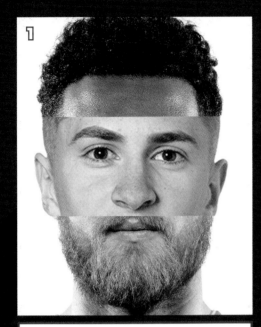

**1**

Hair

Eyes

Chin

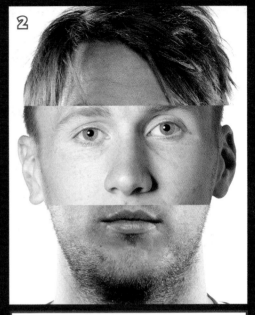

**2**

Hair

Eyes

Chin

**3**

Hair

Eyes

Chin

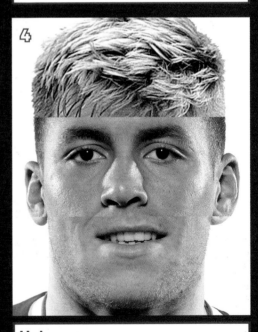

**4**

Hair

Eyes

Chin

Answers on page 60

# Wordsearch

Find the words in the grid. Words can go horizontally, vertically and diagonally in all eight directions.

| | | | | | | | | | |
|---|---|---|---|---|---|---|---|---|---|
| N | J | B | L | E | A | R | F | G | Y |
| O | A | G | O | R | A | M | I | R | P |
| S | R | F | K | T | W | E | G | P | U |
| U | D | T | N | T | R | H | A | Q | R |
| G | I | Z | K | G | O | L | R | E | D |
| R | N | G | M | P | B | V | H | C | U |
| E | E | J | O | E | T | C | O | R | A |
| F | T | L | R | U | T | B | C | N | L |
| G | G | T | D | U | G | M | B | D | J |
| C | Z | B | B | N | X | H | R | F | C |

Albertz          Greig
Butcher          Jardine
Ferguson         Laudrup
Goram            Novo
Gough            Rae

Answers on page 60

# Ibrox Glove Affair

**A number of outstanding goalkeepers have graced the Ibrox turf throughout the years. Here, we take a look at some of the shot-stoppers who have made it into the Rangers Hall of Fame.**

## JERRY DAWSON (1929 - 1946)

### Honours: League – 5; Scottish Cup - 2

Named the Prince of Goalkeepers, Jerry Dawson was a hugely effective last line of defence in the great Rangers team of the 1930s when the club dominated Scottish Football.

Born in Falkirk in 1906, he signed for Rangers in 1929, and by the early 30s had established himself as one of the truly great goalkeepers in the Scottish game.

Dawson was not the tallest player, but like Andy Goram of the modern era he had terrific reflexes and tremendous bravery which enabled him to command his penalty box.

Like many players of his generation Dawson lost the best part of six years to the Second World War, but still managed to play 271 matches for the club winning five League Championships and two Scottish Cup medals as well as being capped 14 times for Scotland.

Unfortunately his final match for Scotland came at Hampden in a narrow 2-1 defeat to rivals England.

His last game for Rangers came shortly after the end of the Second World War. It was against the famous Moscow Dynamo touring team on 28 November 1945. He then joined Falkirk and remained there until he retired from playing in 1949.

After retiring Dawson went on to become the manager of East Fife for a further five years, finally retiring from football in 1955. A legendary Rangers and Scotland goalkeeper, Dawson was voted into the Rangers Hall of Fame in 2002.

## BOBBY BROWN (1946-1956)

### Honours: League – 3; Scottish Cup – 3; League Cup – 2

The first great Rangers keeper of the modern era, he played in 349 games – keeping 109 clean sheets – and had what was then the unusual habit of making sure he turned out with a new pair of white laces in his boots for every one of his matches.

For six years – between August 10th 1946 and April 16th 1952 – he never missed a league game, playing in an astonishing run of 179 matches.

Tall, blond and agile, Brown was the last line in a famous Rangers defence which became known as the Iron Curtain and also featured George Young, Jock Shaw, Ian McColl, Willie Woodburn and Sammy Cox.

He played as a part-timer throughout his Ibrox career, combining football with life as a schoolmaster.

He was ever-present during the historic 1948-49 season when Rangers became the first-team to win the Treble.

In 1947, he won the first of his three full Scottish caps, making his debut against Northern Ireland at Windsor Park.

In May 1956, Brown was transferred to Falkirk for £2,200 but within a year he had retired and later became manager of St Johnstone, guiding them into the top division. In February 1967 he was appointed manager of Scotland, a position he held until July 1971.

## GEORGE NIVEN (1947-1961)

**Honours: League – 5; Scottish Cup – 2; League Cup - 1**

George Niven was a key component of the Rangers team of the 1950s and he won five league titles with them during his time at Ibrox.

Signed from junior outfit Coupar Angus by Bill Struth, he had to bide his time for his break with the club. It wasn't until the final game of the 1951-52 season that he got to play for the team, making his debut in a 2-2 draw with Aberdeen at Pittodrie.

The following campaign however, Niven was an ever-present in the league and his presence helped Gers to a first championship in three years. He was also a Scottish Cup winner that term against the Dons and spent most of the next five seasons as the regular No. 1 having replaced Bobby Brown in the team.

For three years Rangers won nothing but when they took the Scottish crown again in 1956, Niven had once more been a fixture between the posts as he missed just three games.

The title was retained a year later with the goalkeeper playing every minute but in 1957-58 it was Billy Ritchie who was the man beneath the crossbar more often than not.

Niven won his place back after the summer of 1958 and won what would be his final title 34 games later.

The Blairhall-born player didn't enjoy the same success in knockout competitions but he did win a second

Scottish Cup in 1960 against Kilmarnock. Six months later, in the following season, he also got his hands on the League Cup at last as the Ayrshiremen were beaten at Hampden again.

Remarkably, despite making 328 competitive appearances and winning eight major prizes with Rangers, Niven was never capped by Scotland.

## BILLY RITCHIE (1955-1967)

**Honours: League – 2, Scottish Cup – 4, League Cup – 3**

Signed from Bathgate Thistle, Billy Ritchie eventually succeeded George Niven as the regular Rangers goalkeeper in the early 1960s.

Like his predecessor, the Newtongrange-born star could boast an excellent one-in-three shut-out record from his time at Ibrox.

It took Ritchie time to make his breakthrough but by 1961 he was a regular fixture in the side and was quite outstanding at times.

For all his good form with the Light Blues, he only ever won one cap for Scotland – and his first touch in that game with Uruguay was when he picked the ball out of the net.

Ritchie made 340 appearances overall for the club, playing his last match against Aberdeen in 1966 before moving on to Partick Thistle a year later.

One of his greatest games for the club was the 1961 Cup Winners' Cup semi-final at Molineux against Wolves, which helped Rangers to the final.

## PETER McCLOY (1970 – 1986)

**Honours: League – 2; League Cup – 4; Scottish Cup 4; Cup Winners' Cup - 1**

Standing at 6ft 4in, McCloy's towering presence and his birthplace on the Ayrshire coast gave him the nickname 'The Girvan Lighthouse'.

Typical of this giant goalie that he was swapped for two other players in order to bring him to Ibrox. Bobby Watson and Brian Heron were Motherwell-bound to allow Peter to begin his Rangers career in 1970.

The bulb from 'The Girvan Lighthouse' failed to shine for his first couple of games as he conceded two goals in both, as Rangers lost away to Dunfermline and Dundee. He played in seven games in his first season and Rangers only won one of them.

Two games were to have a major effect in establishing McCloy as an Ibrox legend. His clean sheet in the final of the 1970 League Cup earned him his first medal.

However he was to take a more active role in the defeat of Dynamo Moscow in the 1972 European Cup Winners' Cup Final.

Much is made of the modern keeper's ability to start an attack from the back. McCloy was ahead of his time with his long clearances often turning defence into a goal-making opportunity.

It was a long kick from the long man that found Willie Johnston in the position to score Rangers' third in the three-two thriller.

'The Lighthouse' was shining strong in the Centenary Cup final against Celtic. As in Barcelona the score was 3-2 in Rangers' favour.

Stewart Kennedy began to make a play for the No. 1 shirt in 1975. It took three seasons of shirt swapping between the two men before McCloy proved himself the rightful owner. In the 'double' year of 1978-79 Peter never missed a game. He played over 500 games for the club.

## CHRIS WOODS (1986 – 1991)

**Honours: League – 4; League Cup – 3**

Rangers broke the British record transfer fee for a goalkeeper when Graeme Souness paid £600,000 to sign Chris Woods from Norwich City in the summer of 1986. Given that he was vying with Peter Shilton for the gloves with England at the time, his capture was a real coup for the Ibrox side.

Great reflexes and presence made him a formidable barrier and he set the British goalkeeping record in the early part of his Gers career.

After losing a goal to Borussia Mönchengladbach in a UEFA Cup-tie at Ibrox in November 1986, Woods was not beaten again until Hamilton recorded a shock 1-0 win in the Scottish Cup in January 1987. He had kept opponents out for a total of 1,196 minutes, a new British record.

Injury and illness meant he missed large chunks of season 1988-89 and 1989-90 but when fit he was near impenetrable in goal.

The 1990-91 season would be Chris's last in a Rangers jersey. He was an ever-present as the Gers secured a third successive title and the League Cup.

After making a total of 230 appearances for Rangers, Woods left Ibrox in the 1991 close season for Sheffield Wednesday for a fee in excess of £1 million.

## ANDY GORAM (1991 - 1998)

### Honours: League – 5; Scottish Cup 3; League Cup – 2

One of the cult heroes of the nine-in-a-row run, he was voted the greatest Rangers keeper of all time and there are few dissenters.

Goram was a brilliant shot-stopper with magnificent positional sense.

During the 1992-93 season, Rangers enjoyed a remarkable run of 44 games without defeat lasting seven months in both Scottish and European competition.

Crucial to that achievement were the heroics of Goram in goal. He played in all 44 of those games and conceded just 30 goals (in the League it was 18 in 34 matches).

Another way of measuring his outstanding talent is that he kept 107 clean sheets in his 258 games for Rangers. A brilliant record by anyone's standards.

Goram was in goal for the last six of Rangers nine-in-a-row championships. He wasn't tall for a keeper in today's terms, standing at 5ft 11in, but he had superb anticipation, fast reflexes and courage.

Rangers bought him for £1 million from Hibs in June 1991 – one of Walter Smith's first transfer deals – as a successor to Chris Woods. Though it took a while for him to settle in, he completed the remarkable record of playing in all 55 of Rangers' competitive matches during his first season as Rangers won the title and the Scottish Cup.

The next season was the year of the Treble and Rangers' finest run in Europe since the 3-2 victory over Moscow Dynamo in the European Cup-Winners' Cup Final in 1972.

Goram played in all 10 matches in the Champions' Cup, including the two "Battle of Britain" defeats of Leeds,

and conceded just seven goals. He was magnificent as Rangers never lost in that European run and only just missed qualifying for the final.

Another league title beckoned in 1993-94 and Goram won his second League Cup winners' medal with a 2-1 final victory over his old club Hibernian. He won another Championship in 1995-96 and played in the double-winning Cup Final when Hearts were hammered 5-1. Finally, the icing on the cake came when he played in 25 of the league games as Rangers made it nine-in-a-row in 1996-97.

After making 260 appearances, he was given a free transfer in the summer of 1998 and played for Sheffield United, Oldham, Manchester United, Coventry City, Motherwell and Queen of the South before hanging up his gloves.

## STEFAN KLOS (1998 -2007)

### Honours: League – 4; Scottish Cup – 4; League Cup – 2

Affectionately nicknamed 'Der Goalie' by fans, Klos joined Rangers in 1998 after eight seasons with his hometown club Borussia Dortmund.

In his time with the Bundesliga side, he lost a UEFA Cup final to Juventus in 1993 then made up for it with Champions' League glory against the same team four years later.

Klos arrived in Glasgow as Andy Goram's replacement and proved to be a big hit with the Light Blues, winning the championship and the Scottish Cup in his first season.

Those were to be among 10 major honours the German claimed before he left Scotland for retirement in Switzerland in the summer of 2007.

# Training: Behind the Scenes

Josh Windass practices a free-kick in training.

Niko Kranjčar shows some neat control.

Talk about moving the goalposts, Ryan Hardie!

All smiles during training for Danny Wilson and teammates.

Jak Alnwick takes a well-deserved breather.

Carlos Peña having fun as the man in the middle of this drill.

The players pull together during a session.

The players are on their marks, ready for the off in this exercise.

Anyone for head tennis?

# Coach Class

## Joining the backroom team was a natural step for JJ.

Seventeen years after leaving Rangers for the last time as a player, Jonatan Johansson returned to Ibrox as a key member of Pedro Caixinha's backroom team.

The Light Blues' boss was keen to bring someone in alongside him who had an intimate knowledge of the Scottish game and the former Gers striker fitted the bill perfectly.

Having spent three years as Under-20s coach at Motherwell from 2012-2015, the ex-Finland international is well versed in the youth set-up in Scotland and was delighted to be offered the chance to take the next step in his career as Ibrox No. 3.

"It will be a fantastic place to develop myself as well and hopefully I can bring a lot to the team," he said.

"I've lived here for a long time, my wife and son are Scottish and I've worked with Motherwell for three years and you get a good view of youth football in the country.

"Working everyday on the pitch, with top class players, it's a dream for every coach and that's no different for me."

Capped 105 times for his country, Johansson relinquished his position as assistant manager with the Finnish national team to take his place alongside Caixinha and his right-hand man Hélder Baptista, fitness coach Pedro Malta and goalkeeper coach José Belman on the Rangers staff.

"I coached with youth players at Motherwell and with Finland, then stepped up to the first-team with Finland to coach professionals, so I felt I was ready to take the next step," he said.

"Getting into a big club with massive pressure again; working with top class players, but also with the manager and coaches and fitness team - I think this was a natural step for me and the fact it's Rangers is a massive bonus. It was an opportunity I couldn't turn down.

"There are very particular tasks and the manager is very open in the way that he works with the group and we know what is expected from us as coaches in the same way as the players do."

The former striker netted 25 goals for the club in 74 appearances before joining Charlton Athletic in the English Premier League.

He had a loan period at Norwich City before a two-year spell at Malmö in Sweden. He returned to Scotland for brief spells with Hibs and St Johnstone before winding down his playing career at one of his former clubs, TPS, back in Finland.

"I've been back to Ibrox a lot and when I was here as a player the training ground wasn't built yet so coming here is special," added the No. 3, who won two league titles during his Ibrox career.

"It's always great to be at the stadium, too, where there are so many memories."

# RANGERS
## SOCCER SCHOOLS

# Spot The Difference

Study both of the pictures below and use your observtional skills and try to spot the 10 differences between them.

Answers on page 60

# Gers In Europe

Rangers' participation in European football down the years has been marked by an array of memorable goals, both at Ibrox Stadium and further afield. Here we take a look at 10 of the strikes which caught the eye*...

## Rod Wallace V Dortmund
## Uefa Cup Third Round
## November 25, 1999

One of those goals you simply can't help but watch again, and again and again.

On this occasion, a quite wonderful move involving 20 passes from one end of the field to the other ended with Arthur Numan finding the superb run of Jörg Albertz into the left of the box with a classy ball before the German sliced his compatriots open with a beautiful cut-back to Rod Wallace to finish with aplomb.

It was stunning, incisive football which put the Light Blues 2-0 up against an admittedly weaker Borussia Dortmund side than the one which graces their famous yellow-and-black kits these days.

The less said about the second leg the better however, as the Germans came back from the dead to win 2-0 in the Westfalenstadion before going through on penalties.

## Sandy Jardine V Bayern Munich
## Cup Winners' Cup Semi-Final
## April 19, 1972

The late, great Sandy Jardine put Rangers on course for Barcelona with this stunning strike in the opening minutes of the Cup Winners' Cup semi-final in 1972.

With the team having achieved a tremendous 1-1 draw away to the top-drawer Bayern Munich in the first leg, Ibrox was filled to the gunnels with an incredible 80,000 fans turning out hoping to witness some history.

And the place was in sheer uproar with only a minute gone as Jardine picked the ball up in midfield, strode forward in trademark fashion, skipped inside and unleashed a terrific 25-yard drive which nestled in the side netting.

It was quite an astonishing start, and Derek Parlane netted a second later in the half to send Rangers through to the final, and we all know what happened there!

## Bobby Russell V Psv Eindhoven
## European Cup Second Round
### November 1, 1978

Daunting. The only word that can be used to describe Rangers' trip to Eindhoven to face a fantastic PSV side in the European Cup in 1978.

After a 0-0 draw at Ibrox in the first leg, Rangers travelled to face a team who had never lost at home in Europe and pulled off a massive shock.

Already heading through on the away goals rule thanks to Alex MacDonald and Derek Johnstone cancelling out two strikes from the home side, Bobby Russell put the tie to bed with just three minutes left.

Slipped through by a defence-splitting Tommy McLean ball, Russell picked up, sprinted forward to the edge of the box before curling a wonderful finish around the on-rushing goalkeeper.

## Peter Lovenkrands V Stuttgart
## Champions League Group Stage
### September 16, 2003

Seldom has Ibrox gone more crazy in celebrating a goal – and no wonder.

Having toiled for the majority of the match against a highly competent Stuttgart side, Christian Nerlinger had managed to level matters for the Light Blues after Kevin Kuranyi had put the visitors deservedly in front.

A draw would have been no bad result against a team of this quality, but Peter Lovenkrands had other ideas as he netted a wonderful winner just five minutes after Nerlinger's equaliser and with only 11 minutes left on the clock.

Picking the ball up in midfield, the Dane beat two defenders before blasting the ball beyond the impressive Timo Hildebrand in the Stuttgart goal from all of 30 yards to send Ibrox five levels beyond ballistic.

## Charlie Adam V Stuttgart
## Champions League Group Stage
### September 19, 2007

On this occasion the German side visited Ibrox as Bundesliga champions and boasted an array of top talent.

After Mario Gómez had put the visitors in front, it was up to Rangers to find their way back into the match and they managed to do so in some style.

Bursting up the right wing as he so often did, Alan Hutton evaded no less than three challenges before making his way infield.

From there, he played a wonderful ball to Charlie Adam who stepped inside his marker and curled a terrific shot into the top corner from the far corner of the penalty area.

It brought Walter Smith's side back on level terms before a late Jean-Claude Darcheville penalty won the game for the Gers.

## Mark Hateley V Leeds United
## European Cup Second Round
### November 4, 1992

Written off after 'only' beating English champions Leeds United 2-1 in the first-leg at Ibrox, Mark Hateley shut many of his compatriots up with a wonderful strike in the opening minutes of the second leg at Elland Road.

Ian Durrant nodded the ball on for Hateley and, on the volley, he unleashed a thunderous drive beyond John Lukic and into the back of the net.

Greeted with silence inside the stadium given there were no Rangers fans present, it set the Light Blues up to eventually go on to win 2-1 and 4-2 on aggregate to progress to the inaugural Champions League.

## Peter Lovenkrands V Villarreal
### Champions League Round Of 16
### February 22, 2006

It's astonishing and also rather saddening to think it's now over 10 years since Rangers mixed with the very best in Europe in the knockout stage of the Champions League.

Villarreal were truly an excellent side as they proved by reaching the semi-final of the competition, but they were given a real fright by Alex McLeish's side over two legs in the Last 16.

After Juan Román Riquelme had put the visitors in front from the penalty spot, Chris Burke went on a charging run forward before running out of gas just shy of the penalty area.

However, the ball landed nicely at the feet of Lovenkrands who steadied himself before firing a terrific drive beyond Sebastián Viera to draw Rangers level.

The game ended 2-2 and despite one of Rangers' best European performances in the second leg, a 1-1 draw in Spain dumped the Light Blues out of the competition on away goals.

## Steven Whittaker V Sporting Lisbon
### Uefa Cup Quarter-Final
### April 10, 2008

Go on, admit it – if you weren't one of the fortunate ones to be present in the José Alvalade Stadium then you were almost certainly dancing around your living room or local pub when this goal went in.

After an admittedly disappointing 0-0 draw at Ibrox the week before, Rangers were up against it to get a result in Lisbon, but thanks to Walter Smith's tactical masterclass and a little bit of luck, Rangers pulled off a stunning 2-0 win to make it to the semi-finals.

A brilliant counter attack goal finished off by Jean-Claude Darcheville had the Light Blues in front, but it was nothing compared to the clinching second goal scored by Steven Whittaker.

Picking the ball up midway inside his own half, he strode forward at pace, evading three challenges in the process before slotting the ball below the goalkeeper to set the seal on a quite remarkable evening.

## Paul Gascoigne V Steaua Buchares, Ti
### Champions League Group Stage
### November 22, 1995

Rangers' European exploits in the 1990s were probably not as impressive as they should have been given the quality of players at the club's disposal, but Paul Gascoigne provided a moment of real light with this exceptional goal against Romania's Steaua Bucureşti.

With shades of his most famous Rangers goal which he scored against Aberdeen to clinch the league title later in the season, the Englishman picked up the ball in midfield and began to charge forward.

Leaving countless defenders in his wake, he was soon inside the penalty area where he fired the ball into the back of the net to give Rangers the lead.

The night was to end disappointingly, though, with the visitors equalising to claim a 1-1 draw.

## Colin Stein V Dynamo Moscow
### Cup-Winners' Cup Final
### May 24, 1972

'In Barcelona! In 1972! Colin Stein scored one! Willie Johnston two!'

As catchy as the song is however, it only tells you half the story of the greatest night in the history of Rangers Football Club.

Under pressure to deliver, Rangers took the lead when Dave Smith's quick thinking saw him find Stein inside the box with a superb ball over the top before the striker lashed the ball into the back of the net.

The rest, of course, is history as Rangers won 3-2 to bring the Cup Winners' Cup back to Glasgow.

*As selected by rangers.co.uk.

# Where's The Ball?

Can you help the players below figure out which
is the real ball from the match?

Answers on page 60

49

# Dream Debut For Dorrans

## Perfect start to Ibrox career for midfielder

Lifelong Rangers fan Graham Dorrans no doubt spent endless hours dreaming of what his first game for the club would be like.

And it's hard to imagine the midfielder coming up with a better scenario than how his debut against Motherwell at Fir Park unfolded.

The former Norwich City star blasted two goals in his side's first league game of the current campaign as the Light Blues earned a morale-boosting 2-1 victory.

Dorrans took just a few minutes to net his first goal for the club, scoring his second from the penalty spot after the interval.

Looking back on a debut to remember, he recalled: "I was excited before the game. It was something I've always dreamed of since I was a kid.

"But I've been a professional for a long time and I know what you need to do and what it takes to go out there."

The Glasgow-born star had harboured hopes of joining his boyhood heroes for a long time and was understandably delighted when he put pen to paper on his contract in the summer.

Had captain Lee Wallace had his way, however, the midfielder would have been in the dressing-room long before his eventual arrival.

The pair met while on holiday in Florida in the summer of 2016 and the chat quickly turned to football; the seeds sown on a switch to Ibrox.

"After the disappointment of losing the Scottish Cup Final a few of the families were over there on holiday — and so was Graham," said Lee.

"Kenny Miller and I got the conversation going with him and, even at that point, he would have walked it home to sign for us.

"Believe me, we did all we could to get him here even sooner than this summer.

"It couldn't quite happen then but thankfully it's happened.

"That sums the boy up — he was just desperate to come back and play for his boyhood club.

"He wanted to represent Rangers, the side he has loved for so many years, and he wants to feel like he has contributed to making the club successful and closing the gap on Celtic.

"It speaks volumes for Graham that he is here now and he is going to be a fantastic addition.

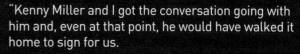

"He believes he can make us better, and I'm sure we are going to see that.

"Graham might feel like he could have achieved more in his career in England. But the fact that he's played at that level for so many years makes me think he'll be quite content with what he's achieved.

"I'm not sure whether rumours linking him with Arsenal at one point were true. But I'm sure he'll feel like he should have won more Scotland caps. But he's in the right place now, he's at the club he loves and we're all delighted that he's on board."

The Rangers skipper knows Dorrans' game well, the pair having been international teammates.

"I played with Graham throughout the age levels, including that Under-19 Euro Final against Spain when he scored our goal in a 2-1 defeat," added Wallace.

"Then, when I made my home debut for the senior side against the Czech Republic in 2010, Graham was there, as cool and composed as ever.

"He got the Man of the Match award that night. He was so calm during a tough period in the game for us.

"The crowd were on us, but he stayed composed, used his touch, picked a pass and used his body well.

"That was a great insight into his quality for me.

"I knew how good he was domestically but not at that level, in a full international game.

"He's got that in abundance and it will be great for how we want to play.

"Graham has always had excellent technical ability in terms of the spaces he picks up.

"He's always got a picture in his head so he's already on the half-turn and knows his next pass.

"He's a clever player, the kind we need."

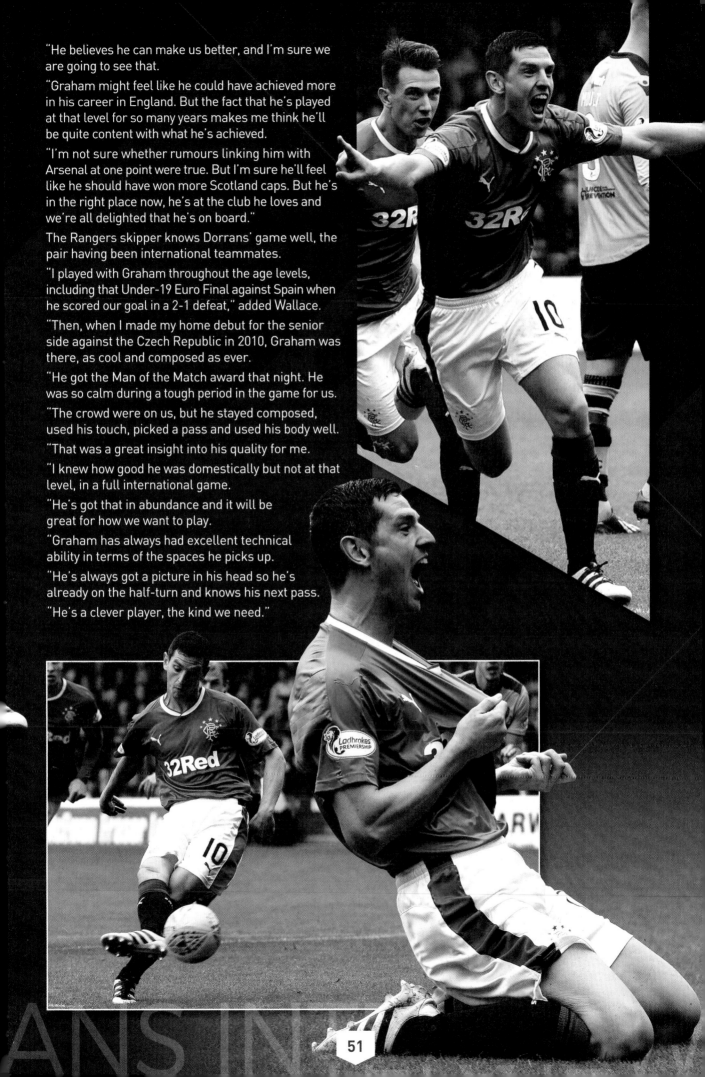

Eduardo Herrera

# Captain Marvels

▷▷▷▷▷▷▷▷▷▷▷▷▷▷▷▷▷▷▷▷▷▷▷▷▷▷▷▷▷▷▷▷

Being captain of Rangers FC is one of the greatest honours in the game. The club has been fortunate enough to have had a number of inspirational leaders down the years and here we take a look at some of the players who have worn the armband with distinction.

▷▷▷▷▷▷▷▷▷▷▷▷▷▷▷▷▷▷▷▷▷▷▷▷▷▷▷▷▷▷▷▷

**Captain 1876-1882**

## Tom Vallance

**Career 1874-1884**

Any team in any sport requires a leader, organiser and inspiration and Tom Vallance possessed all of these qualities when he joined the fledging Rangers and became the club's first great captain.

Indeed, his leadership skills earned him the post of President for six years after his playing days were over.

He was a giant of a man for the period, in the sense that 6ft 2in was extraordinarily tall at that time, and he was a stalwart performer for Rangers in these formative years.

He was in the team that played its first competitive match on October 12, 1874 when they beat Oxford in the Scottish Cup and he was a key figure in the early days.

Vallance played for Rangers for nine seasons at right-back with such distinction that he was made captain in 1876. He won seven international caps between 1877 and 1881, representing Scotland against England and Wales.

Vallance was not only distinguished in his football career. He was a fine athlete, and a Scottish record holder in the long jump. He was also an artist of note, and the Royal Scottish Academy accepted two of his paintings.

▷▷▷▷▷▷▷▷▷▷▷▷▷▷▷▷▷▷▷▷▷▷▷▷▷▷▷▷▷▷▷▷

**Captain 1940-1957**

## Jock Shaw

**Career 1938-1953**

Not for nothing was Jock Shaw known as "Tiger". His tackling had bite and his uncompromising style made him a feared and respected opponent.

Jock, like so many players of his time, missed out on countless honours and international caps because of the war. His 287 games spread over 15 years do not begin to tell the story of his time at Ibrox.

Legendary manager Bill Struth signed Shaw for £2,000 for Rangers in July 1938 from Airdrie and he made his debut at left-back on the opening day of the league season in a 3-3 draw with St Johnstone.

Shaw won the first of his six Scotland caps – all of them as captain – in a 1-1 draw against England at Wembley in April 1947.

Shaw's finest moment however, came in 1949 when he led Rangers to a domestic Treble for the very first time as captain.

Shaw had won four Championships, three Scottish Cups and two League Cups by the time he gave football up. Undoubtedly, but for the war, there would have been more.

## Captain 1965-1978
# John Greig
### Career 1961-1978

John Greig would be THE name on anyone's shortlist for the greatest Ranger of them all.

Men of the stature of Graeme Souness, Sandy Jardine and Ally McCoist have all said Greig was the best and it isn't difficult to see why he is their choice.

It wasn't just his ability, though he was a devastatingly strong and influential player. It was also his passion, his drive, his undeniable will to win that expressed, more than any other contemporary, the essential spirit of what Rangers Football Club is about.

Consider his achievements: captain of his club and of his country; a man who led Rangers to their first European trophy; holder of the club's second-highest number of League appearances with 498 games to Sandy Archibald's 513; second only to Dougie Gray for appearances in all games (including friendlies) with an incredible 859 matches; scorer of 121 goals while playing most of his football in defence or midfield; the only player to have won the Treble an astonishing three times.

But he also had qualities which are becoming rarer to find in modern football. A total devotion to the team and unfailing loyalty to the club.

Greig won the first of his five Championships in 1962-63 (the others were in 1963-64, 1974-75, 1975-76 and 1977-78). The next season, 1963-64, brought the first of those three Trebles. Greig played in every match in all three of the competitions.

His greatest international moment came as captain of the Scotland team which defeated the then-world champions England 3-2 at Wembley.

By 1972 the glory returned as Rangers won the European Cup Winners' Cup, beating Moscow Dynamo 3-2 in Barcelona.

If any player deserves the accolade of Rangers legend it is John Greig. His skill, his determination, and his loyalty through long years of service personify the very essence of what Rangers Football Club represents.

▶▶▶▶▶▶▶▶▶▶▶▶▶▶▶▶▶▶▶▶▶▶▶▶▶▶▶▶▶▶▶◀◀◀◀◀◀◀◀

## Captain 1986-1990
# Terry Butcher
### Career 1986-1990

The Englishman was the foundation upon which the 'Souness Revolution' was built. A brilliant leader and superb defender, he inspired Rangers out of the championship wilderness with the header that won the 1987 title.

Butcher's high-profile capture from Ipswich in 1986 raised the stakes in Scottish football and the England defender went on to become one of the most effective and inspirational captains in Rangers' history.

After a glorious debut season capped with the league-winning goal at Pittodrie, Butcher broke his leg in November 1987, helping Celtic to reclaim the title.

But the England internationalist – capped 77 times – returned the following year to help bring the title back to Ibrox in 1989 and 1990, before he left the club in November that year for Coventry City.

The distinction marks him out as unique, but he was that sort of leader. An accomplished player, he was an excellent timer of a tackle. He also had a fine touch, which made him a careful distributor of the ball once possession was won, and he was commanding in the air.

But it was his calm authority under pressure, a refusal to panic, that transmitted confidence to those around him that made him not only a hugely successful captain but also one of the greatest.

If there is one man who epitomised the effort, drive and skill which led Rangers to nine successive championships during the 80s and 90s, it is Richard Gough.

Captain and great leader of men, Gough was one of only three players to appear in all nine campaigns – Ally McCoist and Ian Ferguson were the others – as well as receiving winners' medals for all nine Championships.

It was Graeme Souness who persuaded Spurs to part with him and he became Rangers' first million-pound man when his signature cost £1.1 million in the autumn of 1987.

It was no wonder, throughout those glory years, that the dedicated player became a role model for fellow players, standing for all that is best in the game. Gough was truly a Captain Colossus.

▶▶▶▶▶▶▶▶▶▶▶▶▶▶▶▶▶▶▶▶▶▶▶▶▶▶▶▶▶▶▶

Rangers career than an entire team of players and he rates his time in Glasgow as the best in his life.

It was little surprise that the sometimes maverick Italian defender earned his place in the Hall of Fame in February 2010, becoming only the fourth non-Briton to do so.

At his best – and he usually reserved this for the important matches – he was a terrific defender who exuded bravery and leadership, tackled fiercely and challenged for every ball as if it was his last moment on earth.

Signed from Fiorentina, there can scarcely have been a more charismatic, passionate and headline-making player in the history of Rangers than Lorenzo Amoruso, whose six years at Ibrox were packed with emotion, excitement, joy and tears.

Appointed captain by Dick Advocaat in the summer of 1998, he went through more experiences in his

The fans loved him and little wonder. He was at the heart of two Trebles in a total haul of nine major honours and he has never hidden his passion for the club, even though he left in 2003.

▶▶▶▶▶▶▶▶▶▶▶▶▶▶▶▶▶▶▶▶▶▶▶▶▶▶▶▶▶▶▶

Smith at the end of season 96/97. The arrival of Dick Advocaat the following year fast-tracked Ferguson's development and he helped Gers to the treble in 1999. A Scotland international, Ferguson became Gers captain in October 2000 and led the team to the Treble in Alex McLeish's first full campaign at the club.

A great leader by example and a terrific passer of the ball, he left Rangers to join Blackburn Rovers for £7.25million having made 482 total appearances for the club. But he returned to begin a new phase of his career with his boyhood heroes in January 2005. He went on to help the club win the league and the CIS Cup in his first four months back at Ibrox and captained Rangers to a cup double in 2007/08 and, of course, the UEFA Cup Final.

Fiery, passionate and superbly skilful, Ferguson was one of the greatest players to feature for Rangers in recent times. He led the Light Blues to a glorious Treble and their 50th title in 2003 and won five league championships in total at Ibrox.

Barry joined the club straight from school and was handed his top team debut aged 19 by Walter

# Friendly Fire

Rangers put the finishing touches to preparations for the League campaign with games north and south of the Border. Here we take a look back at events at Ibrox and Hillsborough, friendlies which saw the Light Blues' fans turn out in their droves to see their team in action.

## Saturday, July 22

### Rangers 1 – 1 Olympique Marseille
### Goal: Kranjčar

Who says pre-season friendlies don't matter? More than 20,000 fans flocked to Ibrox Stadium to see how the team was shaping up ahead of the new campaign.

Those who came along weren't disappointed with the home side matching their illustrious visitors all over the park.

Despite falling behind to a first-half goal, Rangers' heads never dropped and a deserved equaliser arrived 15 minutes from time courtesy of the boot of Niko Kranjčar.

The Croatian was fouled 25 yards from goal but again underlined his class with a superb free-kick into the top right-hand corner.

**Rangers:** Foderingham; Tavernier, Cardoso, Alves (Wilson, 57), Wallace; Candeias (Dálcio, 85), Jack, Dorrans (Holt, 85), Kranjčar (Peña, 76); Miller (Windass, 76), Herrera (Morelos, 57)

**Subs Not Used:** Alnwick, Hodson, Waghorn

**Attendance:** 22, 107

# Sunday, July 30

## Sheffield Wednesday 0 - 2 Rangers
### Goals: Windass, Miller

A huge travelling support was treated to an outstanding display from their favourites at Hillsborough.

Their English Championship hosts proved no match for the Light Blues, with goals in either half seeing Rangers head back up the road with praise deservedly ringing in their ears.

Josh Windass broke the deadlock three minutes before the break before Kenny Miller doubled his side's advantage in the second period to secure a deserved win over a team which narrowly missed out on promotion to the Premier League last term.

**Rangers:** Foderingham; Hodson, Cardoso, Alves, Wallace; Windass (Kranjčar, 74), Jack, Dorrans (Holt, 90+4), Candeias (Waghorn, 89); Miller (Wilson, 86), Herrera (Morelos, 80)

**Subs Not Used:** Alnwick, Dálcio, Bates, Peña

**Attendance:** 20, 739

# Knowledge Quiz

What's your Rangers knowledge like? Test yourself with the 10 questions below then check your answers on page 60.

**1** How many times have Rangers won the league championship?

**2** Who holds the record for the number of appearances?

**3** And how many times did he play for the club?

**4** Ryan Jack joined in the summer from which team?

**5** What nationality is Bruno Alves?

**6** True or False: Jonatan Johansson was born in Sweden?

**7** At what stadium did Rangers secure their famous ninth league title in a row in 1997?

**8** Director of Football Mark Allen left which English Premiership club to join Rangers?

**9** When did Lee Wallace move to Ibrox?

**10** Can you name the year in which Rangers FC was founded?

# STADIUM TOURS

## Get behind the scenes

## Book your
## stadium tour today

**rangers.co.uk** / **0871 702 1972** / **Rangers Ticket Centre**

Calls cost 13p per minute plus network extras.

# Quiz Answers

Check all your puzzle and quiz answers below.

## Page 16. Wordsearch

| | | | | | | | | | |
|---|---|---|---|---|---|---|---|---|---|
| R | X | N | N | H | T | U | R | T | S |
| G | M | C | C | O | I | S | T | M | B |
| A | Q | D | R | R | W | Z | K | P | K |
| S | S | W | D | E | G | T | B | L | L |
| C | S | A | R | T | G | O | M | A | R |
| O | E | D | H | X | G | V | U | E | H |
| I | N | D | P | A | C | D | P | G | D |
| G | U | E | L | B | R | O | W | X | H |
| N | O | L | Z | U | O | P | B | V | Q |
| E | S | L | P | C | S | M | I | T | H |

## Page 34. Guess Who?

**1.**
Hair  Wes Foderingham
Eyes  Myles Beerman
Chin  Jak Alnwick

**2.**
Hair  David Bates
Eyes  Niko Kranjčar
Chin  Danny Wilson

**3.**
Hair  Jason Holt
Eyes  Kenny Miller
Chin  Lee Hodson

**4.**
Hair  Ross McCrorie
Eyes  James Tavernier
Chin  Josh Windass

## Page 35. Wordsearch

| | | | | | | | | | |
|---|---|---|---|---|---|---|---|---|---|
| N | J | B | L | E | A | R | F | G | Y |
| O | A | G | O | R | A | M | I | R | P |
| S | R | F | K | T | W | E | G | P | U |
| U | D | T | N | T | R | H | A | Q | R |
| G | I | Z | K | G | O | L | R | E | D |
| R | N | G | M | P | B | V | H | C | U |
| E | E | J | O | E | T | C | O | R | A |
| F | T | L | R | U | T | B | C | N | L |
| G | G | T | D | U | G | M | B | D | J |
| C | Z | B | B | N | X | H | R | F | C |

## Page 45. Spot The Difference?

## Page 49. Where's The Ball?

## Page 58. Knowledge Quiz

1. 54
2. John Greig
3. 755
4. Aberdeen
5. Portuguese
6. True
7. Tannadice
8. Manchester City
9. July, 2011
10. 1872

Graham
Dorrans

# Where's Broxi?